DECADES

The SEVENTIES

Michael Garrett

STECK-VAUGHN
L I B R A R Y
Austin, Texas

DECADES

The Fifties
The Sixties
The Seventies
The Eighties

**Published in the United States in 1990
by Steck-Vaughn Co., Austin, Texas,**
a subsidiary of National Education Corporation

First published in 1989 by
Wayland (Publishers) Ltd

© Copyright 1989 Wayland (Publishers) Ltd

Edited by Roger Coote
Designed by Helen White

Series Consultant: Stuart Laing
Dean of Cultural and Community Studies
University of Sussex

Consultant American Edition: Jack Nelson
Graduate School of Education
Rutgers University

Library of Congress Cataloging-in-Publication Data

Garrett, Michael, 1955-
    The seventies / Michael Garrett.
        p. cm. — (Decades)
    "First published in 1989 by Wayland (Publishers) Ltd."—T.p.
verso.
    Includes bibliographical references.
    Summary: Discusses the culture and historical events of the 1970s,
including Watergate, the fall of Saigon, skateboards, and reggae.
    ISBN 0-8114-4214-4
    1. United States—History—1969- —Juvenile literature. 2. United
States—Popular culture—History—20th century—Juvenile literature.
3. United States—Social life and customs—1971- —Juvenile
literature. 4. History, Modern—1945- —Juvenile literature. 5. Popular
culture—History—20th century—Juvenile literature. (1. United
States—History—1969- 2. History, Modern—1945- 3. Popular
culture—History—20th century.) I. Title. II. Series.   89-27177
E839.G38 1990   CIP
973.92—dc20   AC

Typeset by Multifacit Graphics, Keyport, NJ
Printed in Italy by G. Canale, C.S.p.A., Turin, Italy
Bound in the United States by Lake Book, Melrose Park, IL

1 2 3 4 5 6 7 8 9 0 Ca 94 93 92 91 90

Contents

Introduction   4

Fashion   6

Pop Music   11

The Media   18

Leisure   23

Youth Cultures   27

Design   32

Images of the Seventies   36

Glossary   46

Further Reading   47

Index   48

INTRODUCTION

Above *Motorists experienced gasoline shortages as a direct result of the oil crisis. Lines at service stations became a familiar sight.*

In many ways the seventies are still too recent to get a clear picture of what happened and why. Our perspective on the twenties, thirties, and even the fifties and sixties is fairly clear. With the seventies it is still difficult to see the picture as a whole.

People like to give names to all sorts of things, and decades are no exception; we talk about the "roaring twenties" and the "swinging sixties," for example. Yet not everyone was a "flapper" in the twenties or a "swinger" in the sixties. In fact, many of the important events and trends in history pass a great number of people by. Nonetheless, these nicknames give us a very rough idea of the character of a decade.

So what is the word to best describe the seventies? There is no doubt that people were more pessimistic than they had been in the previous decade. In the sixties anything had seemed possible. Optimism was high and young people believed they could change the world—through politics, through music, through love and peace. By contrast, the seventies were years of reassessment and doubt. By 1970 many sixties heroes had disappeared. President John F. Kennedy and civil rights campaigner Martin Luther King, Jr. had been assassinated. Musicians Janis Joplin, Brian Jones, Jimi Hendrix, and Jim Morrison were dead through alcohol and drug abuse. The break-up of the Beatles in 1971 was a symbolic end to the decade of hope—and the beginning of an era of worry and disillusionment. On the heels of the swinging sixties came the decade that could be classified as the uncertain seventies.

The oil crisis that began in 1973 formed a background to much of the decade, bringing rising inflation and unemployment to the whole of the Western world. Young people could no longer be certain of finding a job when they left school.

There was an overall lack of direction that characterized the decade. Attention turned away from politics and the belief that "we can change the world." Instead there was a move toward self-analysis: "What am I? Who am I? Where am I going?" People became more concerned with themselves and less with fellow humans.

On a more positive note relationships between the superpowers improved with the signing of the Strategic Arms Limitation Treaty (SALT 1) in May 1972. The Vietnam War finally ended in 1975. People became more conscious of what they were doing to the world they shared with other animals—"Save the Whales" was one of the more noteworthy conservation campaigns of the seventies.

The Women's Liberation movement gained strength. Germaine Greer first published the "bible" of feminism, *The Female Eunuch*, in 1970. During the decade women started to become more independent and more ambitious. Teenage girls were less likely to follow blindly in their mothers' footsteps or accept their "place" in society—usually in the home—without question.

Above all, people still had fun in the seventies. Crazes came and went. Among them were "click clacks"—two balls on a string which you bounced together—chopper bikes, skateboarding, windsurfing, computer games, and roller discos. Changes in fashion and music, especially punk, kept people on their toes. The seventies may have been uncertain but they still had their moments.

Below *Roller discos combined the fun of roller-skating with the energy of disco music. Over-enthusiasm caused many an injury.*

FASHION

The seventies was a decade searching for an image. Various fashion styles were borrowed and adapted from previous eras. There was a fifties revival, inspired by the movie *Grease* in 1978, a twenties revival, and even a "mod" revival reflected in the success of the film *Quadrophenia* in 1979 and "new mod" pop groups, such as the Jam.

Hot pants were fashionable early in the decade. They were really a continuation of the idea of the miniskirt which had been so popular in the sixties. Worn with long "maxi" coats and

Above *Hot pants, often worn with high platform heels, exaggerated the "leggy" look. Many women found the style too revealing.*

thigh-length boots, girls also mixed hot pants with cartridge belts and platform shoes with very high heels. Platforms were designed to make legs look longer and short people taller. They were worn by both sexes, with flared trousers cut to widen from the knee or with loose-legged trousers similar to those worn in the thirties.

The unisex look, which took hold in the sixties, remained popular during the seventies. Men and women dressed more alike than at any other time in this century. Children's clothes became more adult-looking. In the sixties fashion had become geared to teenagers; now even 8- to 12-year-olds could have their own distinctive style.

Denim jeans became almost part of a uniform, and many people from the age of 8 upward had at least one pair in their closet. Jeans were not only unisex; they also appealed to people of all ages and classes because of their comfort and practicality. The denim influence spread to other kinds of clothes. Overalls and denim jackets became fashionable during the decade, and hats, caps, shoes, and belts were also made in denim.

GI Joe and Annie Hall

Military uniforms were combined with other fashionable accessories. Young people liked the strong image of the clothes if not the harsh realities of war. Khaki or camouflage military-style caps were worn with long hair. Military shirts with fake badges were teamed with camouflage trousers and sneakers or fashionable leather boots. The pop group Roxy Music did much to popularize the image with the "GI look," created for them by designer Anthony Price in 1975.

The Annie Hall look, worn by Diane Keaton in Woody Allen's 1977 film of the same name, influenced many women. The style was mascu-

line, featuring tweed jackets worn over high-collared shirts and baggy trousers. The fashion-conscious woman of the late seventies wore her clothes baggy, with several layers one over

Below *Diane Keaton and Woody Allen in a scene from Annie Hall. So-called "masculine" styles were quite popular.*

Below *Fashionable young people wore military-style uniforms and insignia with long hair and jeans for a distinctly un-soldierlike effect.*

Punk was perhaps the most original style of the decade. It was a reaction against glam and so-called "designer" fashions. Punks, usually teenagers, deliberately dressed to shock. They wore "urban garbage," including garbage bags and empty candy wrappers held together with staples. T-shirts and bondage trousers were deliberately slashed. Handcuffs, bicycle chains, and razor blades were used as fashion accessories. The safety pin, sometimes worn through the nose, ear, or cheek, became a powerful punk symbol. Both sexes frequently wore startling make-up. Punks dyed their hair orange, green, or purple, and either shaved it in mohican style or teased it into a multicolored "cockscomb" held in place with hairspray.

Below *Laura Ashley's delicate prints and Victorian designs appealed to women who wanted to look pretty and feminine.*

another—quite the opposite of the miniskirts of the sixties. Peasant styles and fabrics became increasingly popular, too.

Toward the end of the decade there was a reaction against the military look and other masculine styles. Women looked for clothes that were more feminine and flattering than tweed jackets and baggy trousers. Laura Ashley captured the mood with her blouses and dresses in Victorian prints and small flower designs.

Glam and punk

As in previous decades, music had a great influence on fashion in the seventies. Early on "glam" rock led to a craze for glittery, colorful costumes, and hair dyed bright green or orange. Large gangster-style hats and theatrical fox furs became highly desirable items. David Bowie's glam style was widely copied by his fans who were known as Bowie boys and girls.

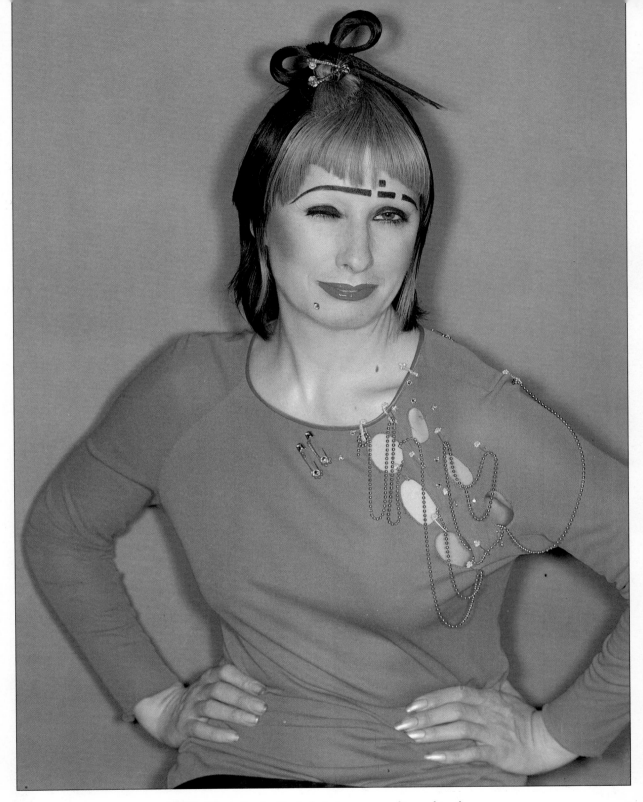

 Above Zandra Rhodes's designs managed to combine the originality and creativity of punk style with a sense of humor.

Above *A late-seventies punk couple photographed in London, complete with flamboyant hairstyles, tattoos, slashed trousers and shirts, and studded leather. It is easy to see why many found the punks' appearance shocking.*

The vast majority of teenagers were not punks, not least because the style was too outrageous for many. Yet punk fashions did have a lasting effect. Designers such as Vivienne Westwood and Zandra Rhodes were inspired by punk ideas, and both continued designing highly original clothes throughout the seventies and eighties.

Hair

Hairstyles were more varied than in the sixties, though not all were as startling as those of the punks. Women had become more independent and less likely to copy styles that did not suit them. Updated versions of the long bobs of the thirties and forties were reintroduced. Farah Fawcett, star of the TV series *Charlie's Angels*, inspired thousands of lookalikes with her rather tousled mane.

Layered hairstyles, like the "Rod Stewart" and the "onion cut," were popular among teenagers. The "wedge," so-called because of its distinctive "flying V" shape, became the style for those who were in the know.

Men's hairstyles started off rather long and untidy but got progressively shorter. By 1978 relatively neat, clean-cut styles with long sideburns were common.

POP MUSIC

The Beatles gave their last live performance in 1970, on the roof of the Abbey Road recording studios in London. The break-up of the group the following year marked the end of an era. The Woodstock generation of the sixties had believed that the world could be changed for the better through music, peace, and understanding, but by the beginning of the seventies the dream was in tatters. The Rolling Stones' 1969 free concert in Altamont, California, was meant to be a celebration of rock'n'roll. In reality, it was a disaster, with raw violence instead of peace. A young man was stabbed to death by Hell's Angel "bodyguards" in front of thousands of spectators. The age of innocence was over.

Above *Lead singer Roger Daltrey as the deaf, dumb, and blind "Pinball Wizard" in the Who's rock opera Tommy.*

Above *Elton John was as famous for his outrageous costumes and his wild eyeglasses as for his undoubted musical talent.*

Art rock and glam rock

At the beginning of the seventies rock music became more self-indulgent. Straightforward rock was out and "art" was in. Following the release of the Beatles' *Sergeant Pepper's Lonely Hearts Club Band* album in 1967, "serious" rock musicians began to see themselves as artists. The Electric Prunes recorded a version of the Catholic Mass; the Who wrote and performed a "rock opera," *Tommy*; and rock bands used symphony orchestras and brass bands more

and more on their albums. The serious tradition was carried on into the seventies by bands such as Pink Floyd, Genesis, and King Crimson.

Glam rock was an extension of art rock but it took itself less seriously. The music was theatrical, and stage performances became a mixture of Hollywood-style glitter and good, old-fashioned rock'n'roll. Performers like Mark Bolan and Elton John created images that owed more to Mae West, Busby Berkeley, and Liberace than anything that had happened in the sixties.

In time glam rock split into two camps. Bands like Roxy Music appealed to a slightly older audience with their more sophisticated sound. T. Rex, Gary Glitter, and Sweet were more "pop." They appealed to younger fans and their singles were very successful on the charts. *Ride a White Swan* by T. Rex was one of the big hits of the early seventies.

Bowie

David Bowie probably had more influence on seventies music than any other performer. He was one of the most original and most copied figures of the decade. He began his career as a glam rocker but changed his image frequently, always a fashion leader rather than a follower. Bowie reacted against the typical "macho" rock'n'roll image. The various characters he created for himself, including Ziggy Stardust, Aladdin Sane, Mr. Newton, and the Blonde Führer, were classless and strangely sexless. It was almost as if he were trying to escape from his own personality. The fantasy world he created appealed to many teenaged fans who felt confused by the "real" world around them.

Facing page *Mime artist, transsexual, genius, urban spaceman, or rock 'n' roller? David Bowie always managed to stay at least one step ahead of the pack and keep everybody guessing.*

Weenyboppers

Children were growing up faster in the seventies than during the previous few decades, and pop fans were younger than ever before. The early seventies saw the emergence of so-called "weenyboppers"—child pop fans often as young as 8 years old.

Pop stars such as David Cassidy, who became famous through *The Partridge Family* TV series, and Donny Osmond had fanatical followings, mainly of very young girls. All the fans needed was a bedroom, a record player, and a friend with whom to share their "secret" love for their favorite pop star. In Britain the Bay City Rollers, a group of young boys from Scotland, were just as popular, and they created a brief craze for tartan clothes. The hysteria at the concerts of these stars was similar to the "Beatlemania" of the sixties.

Manufacturers were quick to see their chance to make a profit out of this new audience. They turned out David Cassidy pillowcases, Donny Osmond watches, and even a Bay City Rollers Monopoly board! Fans' bedrooms were plastered from floor to ceiling with pictures of the young stars.

AOR and disco

AOR, or "adult-oriented rock," was popular throughout the decade, particularly in this country. The American music industry seemed to have lost touch with the teenage market in 1967 with the success of the Beatles' *Sergeant*

Below *The Bay City Rollers perform for adoring young fans. Note the trendy tartan bell-bottoms. Weenyboppers went weak at the knees but the Rollers' fame was short-lived.*

Above *The Grateful Dead still have a cult following in the United States. The devoted fans, nicknamed "Dead-heads," love the marathon concerts up to ten hours long, and some even follow the band to each engagement.*

Pepper album and more adult "California rock" bands including the Grateful Dead, and Crosby, Stills, Nash, and Young. Most American music of the seventies was aimed at college students and the over-25s rather than teenagers. AOR was slick, highly arranged music that appealed to older tastes. Bands like the Doobie Brothers, Steely Dan, and Little Feat had a huge following. Fleetwood Mac's *Rumors* became a best-selling album of the decade.

Disco music became popular on a worldwide scale after the enormous success of the movie *Saturday Night Fever* in 1977. Before this, the music had a "cult" following in New York City dance clubs. Disco sounds later influenced eighties bands including Frankie Goes to Hollywood.

Punk

The Who, one of the giant bands of the sixties, was still singing about "My Generation" in the seventies. But the song's lyrics, "hope I die before I get old," had acquired a hollow ring. Most of the bands that had been so popular in the sixties, including the Who and the Rolling Stones, *were* of another generation, and punks saw them as "fat cats" who had joined the establishment, grown rich, and no longer knew or cared what the average teenager wanted from rock 'n roll.

Punk music was loud and brash, and was played at a breakneck speed that left no time for subtlety. Discordant notes and rhythms were part of the sound. Punk musicians often had little or even no idea how to play their instruments, but that didn't matter. In fact, it was part of the point of punk rock—anybody could do it. You didn't have to be a star to be a member of a band.

Above *Johnny Rotten, so-called because of his bad teeth, led the Sex Pistol's musical assault on the unsuspecting public.*

The Sex Pistols brought the punk movement to the attention of the general public in 1976. They were interviewed on television and took full advantage of the opportunity to be as insulting, abusive, and uncouth as they could. They wanted to shock people and they succeeded. The following morning the newspapers were full of outraged headlines. The image of the pop star had changed dramatically since the sixties interviews with the Beatles. The "Fab Four" may have been insolent but they came across as basically wholesome young men; your mother might accept the Beatles, but she certainly wouldn't like the Sex Pistols.

In fact, punk fashion and music owed its inspiration to New York "cult" bands, such as the New York Dolls, Patti Smith, and the Ramones, who had been around since the late sixties and early seventies. Later, the raw energy of punk music inspired other new wave bands such as the B.52s, Talking Heads, and Devo. Perhaps the biggest success of all was the band Blondie. Their lead singer, Debbie Harry, used her Marilyn Monroe looks to maximum advantage. Known as the "peroxide pixie" because of her

bleached blonde hair, she appeared in teenage magazines all around the world.

As the punk phenomenon lost its shock value and its steam, many bands disappeared without trace. Others, including the Clash and the Damned, adapted or regrouped and survived well into the eighties.

New wave

New wave music followed punk, and retained punk's energy and originality. British bands, such as the Jam, Elvis Costello and the Attractions, and Ian Dury and the Blockheads built up a following by playing gigs on the London pub "circuit." Small, independent record labels, including Stiff and Rough Trade, sprang up to promote them. In the beginning their records were distributed from the backs of trucks or sold at concerts. Just like the punks, new wave bands started to believe that they could manage their own careers. The power of the "majors"—the handful of huge record companies that had dominated the music scene and dictated tastes for so long—seemed to be threatened. In the end the threat was short-lived as the "small-fish" independent companies either went bankrupt or became big fish. The "indie"

Above *The charismatic Bob Marley and his band the Wailers were largely responsible for bringing reggae to the world's attention.*

scene did, however, produce a lot of talent. Elvis Costello's talent and versatility helped him to become one of the most successful singer-songwriters of the eighties. *New Boots and Panties*, an album by Ian Dury and the Blockheads, was one of the wittiest and most successful releases of 1977.

Reggae

Reggae was a result of the influence of American rhythm and blues on Jamaican music in the fifties. It featured a distinctive beat that relied heavily on the rhythm section of bass and

Above *Blondie's British television debut on a popular music program shot the group to instant stardom. The group's music combined the energy of punk with catchy pop melodies.*

drums. Reggae was first adopted by ethnic Caribbean teenagers in Britain during the seventies. Later on the international success of Bob Marley and the Wailers brought reggae to the attention of audiences around the world. Other bands were also influenced by reggae, notably the Police, who combined the style's distinctive beat with more "mainstream" rock melodies to achieve considerable commercial success.

THE MEDIA

The seventies saw a continuation of the trend of the previous two decades—the growth in the popularity of television at the expense of most other media. Increasingly sophisticated technology also made its mark, especially in the areas of television and the movies. This helped to speed up the process by which the media were becoming less national and more global in their focus.

Above *Satellites in space began to beam television pictures all around the world via receiving stations like this one.*

Television

The seventies were dominated by great advances in television technology. Improvements in satellite communications meant that high-quality pictures could be beamed live to most parts of the world in seconds. In 1972 a record one billion people watched the Munich Olympics. The boom in color TV production also greatly increased the appeal of the medium. Video cassette recorders first began to enter the home in the late seventies.

In an attempt to boost viewing figures still further, new television series were aimed directly at teenagers and young children. Fantasy series such as *The Bionic Woman*, *The Amazing Spiderman*, and *The Six Million Dollar Man* were all very popular. Television was becoming truly international, with some series being screened in several countries. *The Bionic Woman*, for example, was made in the United States and also shown in Britain, Ireland, New Zealand, South Africa, Hong Kong, and elsewhere. One of the effects of trying to reach a global market was that programs became highly "packaged," with simple story lines and many visual effects.

Above *The Bionic Man (half man, half machine) oversees the check-up of his female counterpart (the Bionic Woman).*

Sesame Street, *The Electric Company*, and *Mr. Rogers' Neighborhood* became essential viewing for American children. Cartoons or "kid vids" like *Josie and the Pussycats* and *The Harlem Globetrotters* were also very popular.

Some people became worried about the amount of time children spent watching television. The 5 to 15 age group was the fastest growing television audience of all. In 1976, 154 American children aged 4, 5, and 6 were asked "Which do you prefer, television or daddy?" Amazingly, 45 percent of them said they preferred TV.

If children were growing up quicker in the seventies, adult tastes seemed to be becoming more childlike. Another survey conducted in 1980 found that of the top fifteen television programs enjoyed by Americans over 18, more than half were also included in the top fifteen of the 12 to 18 group, including *Family Feud, The Muppet Show, The Dukes of Hazzard*, and *Three's Company*.

In the 1960s broadcasters tended to stay away from controversial topics in fear that they might offend viewers. Politics, sex, and racial issues were generally avoided. In the 1970s some programs began to examine social and political issues in a satiric and entertaining way. *M.A.S.H.*, about a team of American medics during the Korean War, was a good example. *All in the Family* was another popular comedy that confronted the issues which had not been tackled before on television, including racism, feminism, homosexuality, and abortion. And *Kojak*, a popular detective series, dealt with some of the more sensitive issues in crime—drug taking, prostitution, and rape—in a responsible way.

The 1970s saw the birth of the miniseries in television programming. Miniseries were the networks' attempt to incorporate the excitement of the movies and the drama of the "soap op-

Below *More television programs targeted young children. The 5 to 15 age group audience was the fastest growing of all.*

Since the first broadcasts went on the air in 1936 television had always served as a source of entertainment. However, as time went on it played an increasingly important role with its coverage of current events. The Watergate hearings, one of the more noteworthy news events of the 1970s, prompted stations to cancel regularly scheduled programming to broadcast the Senate investigations live.

Radio

Commercial, local radio stations had existed in America since the early days of broadcasting. By the seventies stations catered to particular

eras'' with the sensitive subjects television was beginning to address. ''Roots,'' which chroni-cled the lives of a black slave family, was one of the most popular miniseries of the decade.

Monty Python's Flying Circus, a British tele-vision import, was one of the great comedy suc-cesses of the decade. The zany humor of John Cleese, Michael Palin, and company appealed to all age groups. In the United States the Monty Python brand of humor inspired *Saturday Night Live*, which featured young comics like John Belushi, Dan Ackroyd, and Chevy Chase. All three comics went on to have suc-cessful careers in the movies.

Above *Eric Idle, John Cleese, Terry Jones, and Michael Palin, members of the successful Monty Python team, act silly.*

Above *Special effects influenced the success of blockbuster films such as* Star Wars. *The robots C-3PO and R2-D2 even had fan clubs.*

musical tastes and audiences, playing classical, pop, jazz, rock, country, or easy listening music. This trend toward specialization increased into the eighties. In the early seventies local stations made their first appearance in Britain. Among the first were London's Capital Radio and LBC stations, which began in 1973. Although they were unable to compete with the BBC (British Broadcasting Corporation) in terms of audience figures, they offered specialized programs focusing on local issues and catered to musical tastes not reflected in the pop music charts.

Movies

As in the fifties and sixties, the growing popularity of television continued the decline of movie-going audiences during the seventies. Some people even predicted that the days of the movies were numbered. But they weren't dead yet. Moviemakers responded to the challenge of television by making spectacular films with a fantasy element to appeal particularly to children. They used sophisticated special effects to give life to superbly designed monsters and aliens. *Jaws* was a huge success in 1975.

Star Wars (1977) was the big blockbuster of the decade, followed closely by *Superman* (1978).

Hollywood was dominated during this period by a new breed of filmmaker. Directors like

Steven Spielberg, George Lucas, and John Carpenter were relative newcomers, largely the products of university film schools. They brought a refreshing, new approach to entertainment and a new awareness of young audiences. The box-office success of movies like *Close Encounters of the Third Kind* (1977) and *Star Wars* showed that their approach and cinematic special effects was exactly what audiences wanted.

Nostalgia was a feature of several successful films in the seventies, possibly because viewers felt the decade itself was something of a disappointment. The musical *Grease* (1978), starring John Travolta and Olivia Newton-John, looked back fondly to the fifties, and for a while it inspired a new craze for fifties fashions. *American Graffiti* (1973) painted an affectionate picture of American youth culture in the early sixties, with high school seniors about to leave for the adventures of college or military service.

On a more up-to-date note, *Saturday Night Fever* (1977) brought disco dancing into the limelight. Set in Brooklyn, New York, it shows teenagers trying to escape from their humdrum existence by achieving fame on the dance floor. John Travolta's gyrations were copied by would-be disco kings and queens all over the world.

Magazines

Music papers and magazines such as *Melody Maker, New Musical Express,* and *Rolling Stone* continued to influence teenage tastes and fashion as they had done in the sixties. Fads came and went; heroes were built up almost overnight and often just as quickly shot down. In the sixties, Andy Warhol had predicted that everyone would be famous for 15 minutes; as far as the music press was concerned even this seemed too long.

Below *John Travolta, dancing to the Bee Gees soundtrack from* Saturday Night Fever, *strikes a pose that was to become familiar all over the world.*

New magazines targeting the interests of specific ethnic groups and covering specific musical interests started to appear for the first time. *Black Music*, launched in 1973, was just one example. So-called underground comics like *Fat Freddy's Cat* and *The Furry Freak Brothers* had a cult following. Toward the end of the decade, more sophisticated comics aimed at young girls were introduced. *My Guy* and *Blue Jeans* used photo stories to tackle "serious" teenage issues, although in reality they were all too often of the "boy meets girl" variety.

LEISURE

During the seventies young people were growing up faster than ever before, and were exposed to franker, more open attitudes toward sex. Increasingly racy, television and the movies both contributed to sex ''education,'' if in a rather sensational fashion. The birth control pill first appeared in 1961 but didn't become easily available to younger people until the seventies. In the seventies many

Above *Skateboarding was relatively inexpensive in terms of equipment and offered an appealing mixture of thrills and athleticism.*

youngsters were having sexual relationships at an earlier age than their sixties predecessors. There was still widespread ignorance about venereal diseases and the dangers of "casual sex." The number of one-parent families grew dramatically during this period.

Yet sex was not such a controversial issue as in the days of "free love" during the sixties, when it was used almost as a "weapon" to shock the older generation. Music and fashion, particularly punk, were the weapons of choice in the seventies.

Below *During the seventies, some people worried that prescribing the birth control pill to teenage girls would encourage a more casual attitude toward sex.*

Sports

The entry of children into professional sports was a marked feature of the decade. Gymnasts Olga Korbut, aged 14, and Nadia Comaneci, 13, became household names all over the world when they won Olympic gold medals with near-perfect scores in 1972 and 1976. In 1979 the 15-year-old American tennis player Tracey Austin became the youngest-ever competitor at Wimbledon. Bjorn Borg was the "pop star" of tennis. He won a record four men's singles titles in a row at Wimbledon between 1976 and 1979.

After England's soccer triumph in the 1966 World Cup, Bobby Moore's "golden boys" became national celebrities in England. There was a growth in the popularity of the sport but it was short-lived. In the seventies, attendance at soccer matches was on the decline. For the first time this century more people were playing the game each weekend than watching it! In the stands and around the grounds, violence among soccer fans was becoming increasingly common.

Amateur sports themselves became more "serious" and more competitive. The Little League Baseball Association in the United States was organized along much the same lines as the professional game. In the mid-seventies it was the largest youth sports program in the world.

Jogging became enormously popular, reflecting an increasing awareness of health, and track-suited joggers were seen everywhere. Even President Jimmy Carter joined in the fun, although his enthusiasm must have been slightly dampened when he collapsed during a jog near Washington in 1979.

Below *Russian gymnast Olga Korbut celebrates her gold medal in the women's individual event at the Munich Olympics, 1972.*

Below *Skimming the waves. Windsurfing for pleasure or in the highly competitive races both required skill and strength.*

Skateboarding and windsurfing

Skateboarding was a major seventies craze among children of all ages. It originated in California during the early sixties, but new boards with improved wheels now gave the sport a boost, and it caught on throughout the United States. Britain and Europe followed.

Special interest magazines like *Skateboarder* appeared. The sport developed a language of its own. Advanced riders performed "wheelies," "360s," and "kickturns." Some went "drainpipe riding" for a real thrill. A careless rider was known as a "bingo." Difficult rides were nicknamed "coffin" (riding on your back), the "gorilla grip," and "shooting the duck."

Skateboarding produced its own professional riders. The superstars were mostly American and started skateboarding at a very early age. "Skitch" Hitchcock, otherwise known as the "Airborne Devil," began when he

was ten. At the top, the sport could be very lucrative: in 1976 $20,000 in prize money was given to the winners of a competition in Long Beach, California. For lesser mortals, however, the sport was just a lot of fun.

Windsurfing, like skateboarding, originated in sunny California. Surfing had been popular throughout the sixties, and the addition of a mast and triangular sail added a new dimension to the sport. Windsurfing was exhilarating and fun for all age groups. The fact that it could be done on any body of water added to its popularity. Some expert windsurfers called "hot dogs" performed daredevil stunts.

Variations of the sport included windskating on land, and adventurous types even went ice sailing on skates, reaching speeds of up to 60 miles per hour.

Toys and games

The fifties and sixties had seen the rise of the teenager in terms of spending power, and the

Above *The huge popularity of jogging during the seventies was just one example of an overall trend toward a healthier lifestyle.*

Above *Fantasy-filled arcade video games captured the imagination of would-be space cadets, who happily blasted invading aliens out of the skies.*

manufacturers and advertisers had come to regard them as "targets." In the seventies even 8 to 12 year olds were seen as fair game. Merchandising, the practice of selling articles connected with popular television series and pop and movie stars, became a feature of the decade. There were Donny Osmond T-shirts, pens, and watches, Kojak lollipops, and Muppets toys, and countless dolls and action figures. Star Wars items, developed from the hugely successful movie, sold particularly well.

Toys and games were becoming more sophisticated, and expensive, as the seventies electronics revolution gained speed. Perhaps one of the most successful of the "new" toys was "Simon." Shaped like a flying saucer, it

was a memory game with four colored lights that had to be pressed in the right order. Electronic tank and battle games were followed, toward the end of the decade, by "computer" joystick and paddle games which could be hooked up to a television to provide hours of fun. More sophisticated arcade games like Space Invaders also appeared, testing the player's skill and coordination.

In spite of this technological sophistication, however, the more traditional playthings remained popular, and dolls were still among the most popular girls' toys during the seventies.

YOUTH CULTURES

E ver since the fifties and the early days of the Hells Angels in America and Teddy Boys in England, young people have wanted to stand out from the crowd. Being an individual is not easy, though, especially if, like many teenagers, you are shy and lack self-confidence. The youth cultures that sprang up in the sixties and seventies gave young people a chance to express themselves and have an identity in terms of the way they looked, the music they listened to, and what they were ''for'' and ''against.'' More importantly, belonging to a group of like-minded people was a kind of safety net: why stand out alone when you can stand out together?

Above *The seventies were a melting pot of ideas, old and new. As a result many different tastes and fashion styles gained acceptance.*

Skinheads

In the late sixties, some young people developed a new image. They wore heavy boots, rolled-up jeans, checkered shirts, and suspenders. They shaved off their hair and called themselves "skinheads." During the seventies, they came to be associated with soccer violence, racial attacks, and violence against homosexuals. Skinheads reacted against the hippy values and civil rights activism of the sixties. They were usually working-class boys who exaggerated traditional working-class prejudices. They were often fiercely patriotic, and felt they were defending their country against enemies, so they supported racist organizations such as the American Nazi Party.

To be fair to skinheads, not all of them were racist, but their appearance and some of their actions and attitudes of their leaders gave them that reputation.

Rude boys

In the sixties, Martin Luther King, Jr., and others had argued passionately for racial harmony and equality among blacks and whites. In the seventies there was very little evidence that this dream was coming true. Minority teenagers were still being discriminated against. A background of racism, poor job opportunities, police harassment, and unemployment led some young blacks to escape their hopelessness by looking for an identity of their own beyond the constraints of "normal" society.

In England, rude boys or "rudies" developed from the tradition of the Jamaican "hustler," like the character played by Jimmy Cliff in the film *The Harder They Come* (1972). A hustler was someone who could not find work, or didn't want to, and earned a living through petty crime. Hustlers were cool and streetwise. British rudies and American hustlers associated with this image. They were often unemployed

Facing page *Skinheads cultivated a brutal, violent image—a far cry from the sixties hippies who preached peace and love.*

Below *The Specials, an English band influenced by "rude boy" music and style, had several British hits. Later, the nucleus of the band formed the Fun Boy Three.*

and frustrated, and the "glamorous" rudie image gave them a certain style and identity. They copied the "stingy brim" hats and dark "shades" (sunglasses) worn by hustlers. They smoked marijuana and passed the time listening to ska and reggae music, playing dominoes, and gambling. Some white teenagers adopted the rudie style. In Coventry, England, the Two Tone record label featured bands like the Specials whose music borrowed from Jamaican ska and who had black and white members that took their image from the rudies.

Rastas

Rastas were followers of the Rastafarian religion. They believed that Emperor Haile Selassie of Ethiopia, whom they called Ras Tafari, was a living god, and that one day they would be led to Ethiopia, their spiritual home. This belief was particularly appealing to young blacks who saw Rastafarianism as a way of escaping the harsh realities of prejudice, poverty, and lack of opportunity.

Rastas believed that the illegal drug marijuana, which they called ganga, was sacred. This often got them into trouble with the police. The ''Rastaman,'' with his long ''dreadlocks,'' woolen cap, and Ethiopian colors of red, green, and gold, became an important symbol for seventies black youth.

Above *Rastafarians gave Caribbeans a sense of unity and pride in a shared religion with its own social and moral code.*

Punks

Although it was the Sex Pistols who brought punk to the attention of the general public in 1976, the punk movement had actually started in the early seventies.

Like other groups, punks were trying to find an identity of their own. Punk developed out of British working-class teenage feelings of frustration and of not belonging. Unemployment (the highest since World War II), boredom, life in huge housing projects, and the lack of any real prospects for the future created a subculture with its own deliberately shocking style of music and dress. Meeting places, clothing and makeshift clubs sprang up. Magazines with names like *Sniffin Glue*, *Live Wire*, and *Vortex* were produced by fans. Like punk music and clothes, they were deliberately rough and ready. There was nothing slick about the punk phenomenon.

Punks succeeded in offending traditional, white, middle-class values, which was one of their main objectives. They used fashion, music, and style as their weapons, attracting attention and standing out from the crowd. Perhaps the most important thing about the punks was that they showed it was still possible to be original. Those who had learned the lesson but become bored with the style went on to create other styles. The New Romantics of the early eighties, for example, were often ex-punks.

Below *To many people punks looked as if they came from another planet, but they had an originality that was impossible to ignore.*

DESIGN

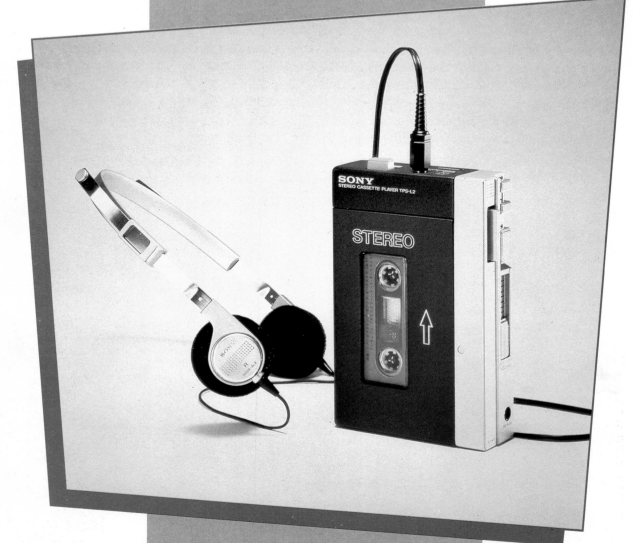

The fifties and sixties had witnessed a building boom resulting from new construction techniques and the need to create inexpensive, functional housing and office space. Huge, boxlike buildings with vast areas of concrete and plate glass were built with little thought as to how practical they were to live or work in. Many were difficult to heat in winter and to ventilate in summer. Huge apartment buildings with dimly lit hallways and elevators frequently out of service became centers for vandalism and crime.

Above Sony launched their Walkman cassette player in 1978. As cheaper models appeared, personal stereos became enormously popular throughout the world.

Postmodernism

In the seventies a legacy of poor planning and bad design had to be dealt with. Many buildings had to be demolished as they were literally falling apart or had become otherwise uninhabitable. On July 15, 1972, the Pruitt Igoe high-rise apartments in Missouri were officially dynamited and razed. Built only twenty years earlier, its design proved so hostile and dehumanizing that people found it impossible to live there. Charles Jencks, a British architect, called this event "the death of modern architecture," and gave a name to the new movement that was to sweep through all areas of art and design—"postmodernism."

The postmodernist movement appeared in the seventies and influenced the design of furniture, textiles, and other consumer products. Behind it lay a rejection of so-called "good taste"—the idea that art and design had to conform to some idea of classical style. Just as punk style was antifashion, postmodernism was antidesign. Postmodernists believed that everything was up for grabs and they freely borrowed ideas from different periods of history. They used unusual materials to create dramatic effects and placed familiar objects in strange surroundings and combinations. They broke the "rules" about what was good taste and what was bad.

Below *Architect Richard Roger's design for the Pompidou Center in Paris was highly controversial. To some it looked more like a chemical plant than an arts center, and people either liked or disliked it a great deal.*

One of the most celebrated examples of postmodernist architecture is the Pompidou Center in Paris built by Richard Rogers in 1978. One of the most original is the Best Products Showrooms in Houston, Texas, built in 1975 by the SITE Architects group.

Design in miniature

The microelectronics revolution had far-reaching consequences for familiar and not-so-familiar household objects. Electrical components were made smaller and smaller, and this meant that many electronic devices could also be smaller. Clive Sinclair invented the first pocket calculator in 1972 and the first miniature TV followed in 1975. In 1978 Sony launched their "Walkman" cassette player. The invention of the silicon chip enabled computer manufacturers to greatly reduce the size of their machines, and the first portable computer became available in 1977.

Habitat and high-tech

In the mid-seventies Terence Conran's "Habitat" chain of shops started to have a real influence on the type of design found in middle-class British homes. By 1975 there were 12 shops around the country, one in Paris and one in New York. Habitat in England and Conran's in America sold good-quality, well-designed furniture and kitchen equipment, influenced by French and Scandinavian designers. In many ways Conran was responsible for making design accessible to more people.

High-tech emerged in the seventies and its popularity carried on well into the next decade. It was a design style for the home, heavily influenced by the clean lines and simplicity of industrial design. The practice of converting large "lofts" or warehouses into family homes started in New York City. These very spacious apartments were particularly suited to the high-

Above *Cambridge-based scientist Clive Sinclair was one of the first people to realize the potential of miniaturization. His pocket calculator was the first in a long line of innovative products.*

Above *New York subway trains were painted both inside and out by aspiring young street artists. To most people, however, it was simply vandalism, and subway riders would ultimately bear the cost of cleaning it up.*

tech look. Industrial furniture, steel shelving, factory-style lights, and hard-wearing rubber flooring gave them a pleasing simplicity and made maximum use of space. High-tech was supposed to look and feel empty. In many ways the new designs were a reaction to the over-elaborate style and decor found in the homes of the forties and fifties.

Spray-can art

In the seventies graffiti became increasingly common. It also came to be regarded by some as an art form. Whereas it had once been confined to neighborhood walls and bus shelters, young ''artists'' in New York discovered that subway trains made excellent movable ''canvases'' for their designs. They adopted nick-

names or ''tags'' that were recognizable to their friends if not to the police. ''Taki 183,'' ''Crash,'' ''Daze,'' and ''SAGO'' became familiar ''signatures'' to New York commuters, and in some cases styles were recognizable without signatures.

Some of the more talented ''artists'' like Vaughn Bode went on to hold major public exhibitions of their work. However, not all graffiti was art. Most was little more than crude vandalism. The New York subway system and other agencies were forced to spend vast sums of money to clean graffiti from their property, and to try to develop graffiti-proof trains.

IMAGES OF THE SEVENTIES

Bloody Sunday

Against a continuing background of violence from political and religious unrest in Northern Ireland, Brian Faulkner, the prime minister, introduced internment without trial in 1972. This meant that anyone suspected of having committed a violent crime could be held indefinitely without trial. Hundreds of suspects were rounded up and questioned by the security forces. On Sunday, January 30, a large demonstration against the policy of internment in Londonderry was broken up when British troops fired on protest marchers, killing thirteen of them. This day became known as ''Bloody Sunday.'' Not long afterward the Northern Irish Parliament at Stormont was suspended and the province was administered by direct rule from London.

Above *British troops round up protesters in Londonderry, Northern Ireland. The introduction of internment without trial caused a great deal of anger and resentment.*

The Munich Olympics

The seventies saw a dramatic increase in acts of terrorism. Groups like the Red Army Faction and Black September sought to achieve political goals through acts of violence often directed at innocent civilians. The most shocking incident occurred during the Olympic Games in Munich in September 1972, and was carried out by eight terrorists from the Black September organization. They shot two Israeli athletes dead and took nine hostages. The terrorists demanded the release of 200 Arab hostages who were being held captive by the Israelis.

The West German authorities negotiated with the terrorists and moved them and their hostages to a nearby airport, apparently agreeing to fly them to a friendly Arab country. But German marksmen were lying in wait. In the shoot-out that followed, all the hostages and five terrorists were killed.

Below *The bodies of the murdered Israeli hostages are flown home from the 1972 Munich Olympics. The world was shocked by the terrorists' fanatical disregard for innocent lives.*

The Concorde

The Concorde, the world's first supersonic airliner, was a joint Anglo-French project which took over 20 years to get from the drawing board into the air. Its elegant shape and "droop snoot" nose made it one of the most distinctive, and many would say the most beautiful, airplanes ever built. The Concorde finally came into service on January 21, 1976, and became the epitome of luxury trans-Atlantic air travel. But it was costly to build and to run, and some countries objected to the noise it made as it broke the sound barrier. Very few Concordes were sold, and no more were built after 1979.

Below *Opposition to the Concorde from environmental groups led some countries to ban the plane from flying over them.*

Muhammad Ali

Cassius Clay, who later changed his name to Muhammad Ali after becoming a Muslim, was arguably the greatest heavyweight boxer of all time. He first won the world heavyweight title in 1964 when he was 22, taking it from Sonny Liston. Ali's arrogance (his catch phrase was "I'm the greatest"), his sense of humor, and above all his superb, seemingly effortless boxing ability—he could "float like a butterfly and sting like a bee"—made him world-famous.

His religious convictions led him to refuse to serve in the U.S. Army during the Vietnam War. As a result he was deprived of his title for three years between 1967 and 1970. During the seventies he regained the title twice, the only heavyweight ever to do so.

The first test-tube baby

On July 25, 1978, Louise Joy Brown was born in Oldham General Hospital, in England. She was the first baby to be conceived outside its mother's womb.

Her mother, Lesley, had once been told that she could never have a child. The successful birth was the result of a collaboration between Oldham gynecologist Patrick Steptoe and two Cambridge doctors, Robert Edwards and Barry Bavister. They developed a technique by which an egg taken from a woman's ovary could be fertilized in a test-tube by sperm from a man, and then returned to a womb to grow. Little Louise, a normal, healthy baby, gave new hope to childless women. However, questions about these new techniques would create controversy and moral dilemma in the eighties.

Above Muhammad Ali triumphed over "Smokin'" Frazier in the last two of their three world title bouts, taking revenge for his defeat in their first match.

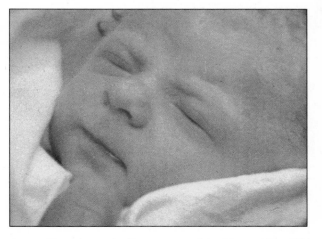

Above Louise Joy Brown—normal, healthy, and blissfully unaware of her historical and medical importance as the world's first test-tube baby.

Watergate

The Watergate scandal of the early seventies shocked people in the United States and around the world. At first it seemed little more than an example of petty corruption. In June 1972, an election year, five men were arrested after breaking into the Democratic Party headquarters in the Watergate building in Washington, D.C. They were caught trying to plant electronic surveillance equipment and photographing sensitive documents. Richard Nixon, the Republican president, denied that he or any of his staff were involved in what he called this "reprehensible activity." However, an investigation by the *Washington Post* newspaper indicated otherwise and the Watergate burglars were proved to be connected to the Nixon administration. Nixon himself refused to appear before a Senate Select Committee or to release sensitive tape recordings that may have implicated him in the scandal. Although Nixon had been reelected by a landslide in 1972, as the scandal unfolded, his popularity plummeted. People were shocked that their president was apparently dishonest. In August 1974 Nixon finally admitted withholding important information and offered his resignation.

Above *President Nixon taped most of his White House conversations and these tapes later implicated him in the Watergate scandal.*

Nicaragua

Anastasio Somoza first came to power in the Central American country of Nicaragua in 1967. The Somoza regime swiftly acquired a reputation for corruption, extortion, and violence against all those who opposed it. Somoza himself reputedly accumulated a fortune of some $500 million while in office. In 1973, public discontent grew when it became clear that Somoza had "diverted" aid sent to help victims of a devastating earthquake to swell his already bulging coffers. Support for the Sandinista National Liberation Front (SNLF)—named after Augusto Sandino, a national hero who had been murdered by Somoza—grew rapidly. A bloody civil war broke out in which 40,000 Nicaraguans died and 75,000 lost their homes. The war ended in 1979 when Somoza fled to neighboring Paraguay, where he died a short time later. Shortly thereafter, the Sandanista directorate installed a Communist government.

Facing page *Anastasio Somoza, as one of the most ruthless dictators in South America, relied heavily on the loyalty of the Nicaraguan Army.*

The fall of Saigon

The Vietnam War, one of the longest in modern history, first started in the late fifties. United States involvement began in 1962 when President John F. Kennedy sent 4,000 American advisers, and by 1972, 350,000 American troops were involved in the guerrilla war on the side of South Vietnam.

The war became increasingly costly and unpopular. What had initially been seen as a crusade against the evils of Communism (in the form of the North Vietnamese) became a war in which the United States appeared to be in a ''no-win'' situation.

The United States finally decided to cut its losses and the last American troops left Vietnam in 1973. In July 1975, Communist troops entered Saigon, the South Vietnamese capital. The few remaining American personnel had earlier been hurriedly airlifted out by helicopter amid scenes of panic and fear. The war was over but the United States had paid a high price—50,000 American soldiers had been killed.

Below *America's withdrawal from Vietnam caused panic as thousands of South Vietnamese fled from Communist troops. Later, many desperate refugees known as ''boat people'' took to the sea.*

Mass suicide at Jonestown

In the mid-seventies the "Reverend" Jim Jones founded a religious commune in Guyana. He moved his followers from San Francisco to the South American jungle where he established the People's Temple. Cut off from the outside world, he was able to present himself to the members of his cult as a kind of god. Those who refused to accept his "divinity" were murdered. Reports of corruption and violence that reached the outside world led to an investigation of the cult by a group of United States' politicians and journalists. They were attacked by Jones's fanatical followers and four were shot. Realizing that his days were numbered, Jones ordered his followers to commit mass suicide by poisoning themselves. Those who refused to do so were shot. In all, 913 members of the Temple died in November 1978, including Jones himself.

Three Mile Island

In the seventies nuclear power was seen by many people as a cleaner, cheaper solution to the growing energy crisis. Others expressed concern about the dangers of potentially catastrophic accidents in nuclear power stations. One such accident occurred at the Three Mile Island nuclear plant near Harrisburg, Pennsylvania, on March 28, 1979. A small amount of radioactive gas was released into the atmosphere. The population of Harrisburg and the surrounding area was evacuated. Fortunately, no one was seriously hurt but it became obvious that nuclear power plants were not as safe as their proponents claimed. A Nuclear Regulatory Commission study later revealed that the reactor at Three Mile Island was within 60 minutes of a "meltdown" which could have caused thousands of deaths. This accident caused many to rethink nuclear power.

Above *Antinuclear protesters have cited the near-miss of disaster at Three Mile Island in Pennsylvania as a warning of the potential dangers that are associated with nuclear power.*

Idi Amin

Idi Amin was an ex-army sergeant who rose to become the self-appointed President for Life of Uganda during the years 1971 to 1979. His enormous physique and "unconventional" style—he had 6 wives and 20 children—made him a figure of fun to much of the Western world.

Inside Uganda, however, people weren't laughing at Amin. He ruled with appalling savagery. During his time in office more than 350,000 Ugandans were murdered as "political opponents." It was one of the bloodiest chapters in Ugandan history.

Revolution in Iran

The year 1971 marked the 2,500th anniversary of the Persian monarchy. At that time the Shah of Iran could have been forgiven for believing that his position on the throne was secure. His handling of Iran's economy had created enormous wealth and the general standard of living had improved considerably since he came to power in 1953. All should have been well. However, other forces were at work.

Iran is an Islamic country and its people are deeply religious. The mullahs—Islamic religious leaders—objected to the Shah's "modern" approach. They preached Islamic fundamentalism and a return to the teachings of the Koran. In 1979 the 79-year-old Ayatollah Khomeini returned to Iran from exile in Paris and was given an ecstatic reception. He demanded the removal of the Shah and a return to pure Islamic values. In January the Shah was forced to bow to public pressure and he left the country.

Left *Many Westerners regarded Idi Amin as a figure of ridicule, but beneath his pompous self-importance lay a brutal dictator. In 1979 Amin fled when his country was invaded by Tanzanian troops and Ugandan exiles.*
Facing page *Many fervent supporters greeted the Ayatollah Khomeini on his return to Iran.*

GLOSSARY

AOR (adult-oriented rock) A term used to describe rock music (usually American) that is more sophisticated and more highly arranged than the normal pop single.

Bluebeat (and ska) Music that originated in Jamaica and was brought by Caribbean immigrants in the fifties to Great Britain and later to the U.S.

Bondage trousers Punk-style trousers decorated with many zippers, straps, and chains which were often deliberately slashed as well.

Busby Berkeley A 1930s director of Hollywood musicals who was known for his lavish dance routines and set designs. Berkeley's style inspired glam-rockers such as Elton John and Brian Ferry.

Civil Rights Rights, based on the principle of equality, that belong to everyone in a free society, such as the right to vote and the right to a fair trial. The civil rights movement aimed to win these rights for black citizens.

Communism A political theory aiming to establish a society where the major enterprises such as factories, mines, farms, and stores are owned by all the citizens rather than a class of wealthy people. Each person should work at his or her ability and receive according to his or her need. In practice, Communist societies have tended to create powerful state authorities to control those enterprises.

Contraceptive A device used to prevent pregnancy. The birth control pill first became available to women in the sixties.

Cult In fashion terms, a small group of people who appreciate the same, usually offbeat style and group together to be different from more "mainstream" fashions. In religious terms, members of a sect, often blindly following one powerful individual.

Divinity The state of being godlike.

Droop-snoot The name given to the long, pointed nose of the Concorde, which can be lowered during take-off and landing to give the pilot better visibility.

Feminism The movement aiming to win full rights and respect for women in society, and to celebrate the special qualities of the female sex. Also known as "Women's Lib."

Flapper A name for a fashionable young woman of the twenties.

Functional Something designed to work efficiently rather than just to look attractive.

Gig A pop or jazz music concert.

Graffiti Drawings, names, and messages scribbled or painted on walls, advertising posters, etc. In the seventies New York's subway trains became targets for graffiti "artists." Many felt it was not art but simply vandalism.

Hell's Angels Groups identified with high-powered customized motorcycles and sometimes associated with gang violence.

High-tech A design style that uses industrial-style objects and furnishings in the home to emphasize simplicity and space.

Indie Short for independent; a word used to describe the small record labels that sprang up in the seventies to promote new wave bands. The few "indies" that survived generally made it big.

Inflation The rate at which the price of goods and services increases. When inflation is high, prices rise very quickly. If wages don't go up as quickly as prices, times get tough for many.

Internment Detaining or imprisoning people, especially during wartime or times of revolution.

Macho A word to describe fashions and behavior that make men look tough and aggressive; from the Spanish word *machismo*.

Marijuana An illegal drug derived from the hemp plant.

Mods Fashion-conscious working teenagers who emerged in England during the early sixties.

Nostalgia Looking back to the past with affection, in the belief that life was better then than it seems to be now.

Oil crisis The worldwide economic crisis brought on when Arab oil-producing nations doubled the price of oil and cut its production. Many countries experienced a shortage of oil, industrial production fell, and inflation and unemployment rose sharply.

Optimism A tendency to expect the best.

Patriotism Pride in one's own country. Although skinheads frequently claimed to be patriotic, this often became an excuse for racial hatred and violence.

Pessimistic People who always expect the worst are said to be pessimistic.

Unemployment The condition of being out of work.

Unisex Clothes designed to be worn by either sex.

Venereal disease (VD) Disease passed from one person to another during sexual intercourse.

Woodstock A town in New York State, where a huge, outdoor, rock music festival was held in 1969 that in many ways came to symbolize the hopes and dreams of the sixties youth culture.

FURTHER READING

America in Search of Itself: The Making of the President 1956–1980, Theodore H. White (Harper, 1982)

America Inside Out: At Home and Abroad from Roosevelt to Reagan, D. Schoenbrun (McGraw-Hill, 1985)

Chronicle of the 20th Century (Chronicle Pub., 1987)

Televison 1970–1980, Vincent Terrace (A.S. Barnes, 1981)

Television: The First Fifty Years, Jeff Greenfield (Abrams, 1977)

The United States in the Vietnam War, Don Lawson (Crowell Jr. Books, 1981)

Yesterday & Today: A Dictionary of Recent American History, Stanley Hochman (McGraw-Hill, 1979)

Picture Acknowledgments

Barnaby's Picture Library 10, 18, 24t, 25t, 25b, 27; Camera Press 30 (Lennox Smillie), 35 (Willy Spiller), 40 (Ollie Atkins), 44 (Richard Lindley), 45 (J. Haillot/L'Express); Daily Telegraph Colour Library 3 (Patrick Ward); Kobal Collection *cover, lower right,* 7, 19, 21 (Lucasfilm Ltd); Photri 8t, 20t, 23, 43t; Popperfoto *cover, upper right,* 24b, 36, 37; Redferns 12, 14, 16b; Rex Features *cover, left,* 4, 5, 6, 11, 13, 15, 16t, 22, 26, 28, 29, 31, 39t, 39b, 42; Sony UK 32; TOPHAM 8b, 9, 17, 20b, 33, 38, 41, 43b.

INDEX

Ali, Muhammad 38, 39
American Graffiti 22
Amin, Idi 44
Annie Hall 7
Architecture 32–34
Ashley, Laura 8

Bay City Rollers 14
Beatles 5, 11, 12, 14, 16
Birth control pill 23, 24
Black September group 37
Blondie 16, 17
Bloody Sunday 36
Bolan, Mark 12
Bowie, David 8, 12
Britain 17, 19, 21, 24, 25, 29, 30, 34, 36, 39

Carter, President Jimmy 24
Cassidy, David 14
Close Encounters of the Third Kind 22
Clothes 6–10, 29
Concorde 38
Conran, Terence 34
Costello, Elvis, and the Attractions 16, 17
Crosby, Stills, Nash, and Young 15

Deadheads 15
Devo 16
Discos 15
Doobie Brothers 15
Drugs 29, 30
Dury, Ian, and the Blockheads 16, 17

Fleetwood Mac 15

Genesis 12
Glam rock 8, 12
Graffiti 35
Grateful Dead 15
Grease 6, 22
Greer, Germaine 5

Hairstyles 8, 10
The Harder They Come 29
High-tech 34–35

"Indie" record labels 16–17
Inflation 5
Iran 44
Israel 37

Jam 6, 16
Jaws 21
Jogging 24, 25
John, Elton 12
Jones, "Reverend" Jim 43

Kennedy, President John F. 5, 42
Khomeini, Ayatollah 45
King Crimson 12
King, Martin Luther, Jr., 5, 29

Lucas, George 22

Magazines 22, 25, 31
Marijuana 29, 30
Marley, Bob, and the Wailers 16, 17
Merchandising 26
Microelectronics 34
Movies 21–22
Munich Olympics (1972) 19, 24, 37
Music 11–17, 24, 29, 30, 31

New Wave 16
Nicaragua 40
Nixon, President Richard 40
Northern Ireland 36

Oil crisis 4,5
Osmond, Donny 14, 26

Pink Floyd 12
Pocket calculator 34
Police 17
Pompidou Center 33, 34
Postmodernism 33–34
Punk 5, 8–9, 10, 15–16, 24, 30–31, 33

Racism 29
Radio 20–21
Ramones 16
Rastafarians 30

Reggae 17, 29
Rhodes, Zandra 9, 10
Rogers, Richard 33, 34
Roller discos 5
Rotten, Johnnie 16
Roxy Music 7, 12
Rudies 29

SALT 1 Treaty 5
Sandinista National Liberation Front 40
Satellite communications 18, 19
Saturday Night Fever 15, 22
Sex 23–24
Sex Pistols 16, 30
Silicon chip 34
Sinclair, Clive 34
Skateboarding 5, 23, 25
Skinheads 28, 29
Somoza, Anastasio 40
Sony Walkman® 32, 34
Specials 29
Spielberg, Steven 22
Sports 24
Star Wars 21, 22, 26
Superman 21

Talking Heads 16
Television 18, 19–20
Terrorism 37
Test-tube baby 39
Three Mile Island 43
Tommy 11, 12
T. Rex 12

Uganda 44
Unemployment 5, 29, 30
United States 14–15, 19, 20, 22, 24, 25, 33, 34–35, 40, 42, 43

Vandalism 32, 35
Video games 26
Vietnam War 5, 38, 42

Watergate 20, 40
Weenyboppers 14
Who 11, 12, 15
Windsurfing 5, 25
Women's Lib 5